CW01467716

How to Prepare for GDPR and Improve Digital Channels in a Post GDPR World

An introductory summary by:

**Maurice 'Big Mo' Flynn FCIM CMPRCA MEng
Cantab**

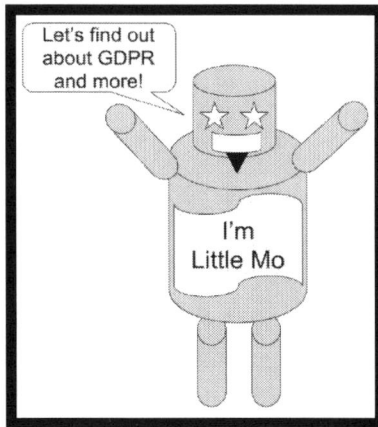

Best wishes for your GDPR journey Kelly!

Maurice Big Mo Flynn

About the Author

Maurice 'BigMo' Flynn FCIM CMPRCA MEng
Cantab

Maurice has **delivered learning events on these and related topics** for many of the biggest training companies in the UK, including the **CIM, ISMM, E-consultancy, DMA/IDM, DMI, British Council, IAB** and more. At the **DMA/IDM** Maurice (and others) supports the expert council hubs which help members optimise their marketing as well as prepare for GDPR. He also participated in the **ICO's public GDPR consultation process**. Over 30 years Maurice has trained **thousands of people at hundreds of companies**, including **Oracle, BBC, P&G and Google**. He is married to his business partner Antoaneta and they have two young boys.

Copyright © Maurice 'Big Mo' Flynn 2017-18 (Open Doors Ltd.)
GDPR Training Events - Reviews - Feedback

Testimonials

"Our members took a lot out of your logical GDPR approach." **Hotel Booking Agents Association (HBAA)**

"Maurice has been supporting the DMA Email Council hubs for 2+ years." **Direct Marketing Association**

"Maurice is selected to bring his expertise to the PRCA Council in 2018." **Public Relations and Comms Assoc.**

"Maurice has successfully trained 100's of our clients." **Cambridge Professional Academy (CIM)**

"Helps you understand what is relevant to your situation. I can't recommend highly enough." **WeAreGecko.co.uk**

"Fantastic grounding in (GDPR) data protection." **YGAM**

"Excellent, well structured & informative." **FinsSwimClub**

"Quality info in an easy to read & digestible format." **EkuaB.**

"Most clarity I've received from anywhere." **Armitt.co.uk**

Copyright © Maurice 'Big Mo' Flynn 2017-18 (Open Doors Ltd.)
GDPR Training Events - Reviews - Feedback

"Cuts through the jargon and red tape, giving a practical focus on the steps to take." **Lenleys.co.uk**

"Our go to GDPR expert." **BreatheAgency.com**

"Helped with re-permissioning & privacy policy." **SunnyD**

"Intelligent approach to GDPR." **TMWUnlimited.com**

Copyright © Maurice 'Big Mo' Flynn 2017-18 (Open Doors Ltd.)
GDPR Training Events - Reviews - Feedback

Dedications and more ...

These are the **collective opinions of Maurice 'Big Mo' Flynn** based on 30 years of relevant working experience and a **lifetime of learning and working with like minded experts**. They are therefore **not meant to be 100% perfect for everyone** - they are **simply meant to be generally useful!** They are especially relevant for **companies with limited resources** who are looking for a common sense approach. **Disclaimer: I'm not a lawyer so cannot dispense legal advice!**

Dedicated to my mother, sister and brother who never stop moving forward. Plus my wife and sons who get me out of bed in the morning, whether I want to or not. :)

Copyright © Maurice 'Big Mo' Flynn 2017-18 (Open Doors Ltd.)
GDPR Training Events - Reviews - Feedback

Contents

Copyright © Maurice 'Big Mo' Flynn 2017-18 (Open Doors Ltd.)
GDPR Training Events - Reviews - Feedback

Copyright © Maurice 'Big Mo' Flynn 2017-18 (Open Doors Ltd.)
GDPR Training Events - Reviews - Feedback

Part 1- Intro to GDPR Prep

Guess What?

Be warned ... **I'm not a lawyer** so won't be giving legal advice! This course is in fact curated from the **still evolving advice of experts** e.g. the ICO (Information Commissioner's Office). Overall I wanted to develop an approach that is "**as simple as possible**" and delivers a "**to do checklist**" applicable for all. Do let me know if I succeeded!

But First ... [Video Link]

Let's start with you ... **What's your objective?**

Feel free to scribble below...

My Objective:

_____

What have you heard about GDPR? There is a lot of confusion, partly because some of the rules will **ultimately be clarified in the law courts**. But we can't

Copyright © Maurice 'Big Mo' Flynn 2017-18 (Open Doors Ltd.)
GDPR Training Events - Reviews - Feedback

wait around for that! We aim here to **focus on essential business needs** as far as possible. P.S. In our events we like to **keep things interactive** and stimulating i.e. questions are good and opinions are welcomed.

Expert Recommendations:

- ☒ Key principles are **1. Privacy Management Ownership:** i.e. relevant activities are embedded throughout the organisation; **2. Responsibility:** i.e. activities are implemented and maintained; **3. Evidence:** i.e. this activity produces documentation that shows accountability and compliance.

- ☒ **Fines of up to €20 million or 4% of total worldwide annual turnover** of the preceding financial year, but compliance efforts will mitigate (Art.83). **Liability to 'data subjects'** (who's personal data is involved) depends on compliance and proof of effect (Art.82).

- ☒ **Existing related law**: Employment contracts (Art.88), Freedom of Info Requests (Art.86),

Copyright © Maurice 'Big Mo' Flynn 2017-18 (Open Doors Ltd.)
GDPR Training Events - Reviews - Feedback

National ID's (Art.87), Freedom of Expression (Art.85).

Copyright © Maurice 'Big Mo' Flynn 2017-18 (Open Doors Ltd.)
GDPR Training Events - Reviews - Feedback

Step 1: Raise awareness

How?

We need to raise awareness of GDPR amongst our **senior management first** as they are key to making change happen. We then need to raise awareness - in an organised and documented way - amongst our **employees and close partners, who come into contact with personal data**. Finally we need to raise **general awareness of GDPR for all our people,** to minimise the risks of human error as well as document our commitment and compliance.

Start with the basics ... [Video Link]

The General Data Protection Regulation (GDPR) is a **regulation (i.e. legal)** by which the EU governing bodies will **strengthen and unify personal data protection**. It becomes applicable from **25th May 2018** and involves all people

Copyright © Maurice 'Big Mo' Flynn 2017-18 (Open Doors Ltd.)
GDPR Training Events - Reviews - Feedback

resident in **the EU and their personal data**. Therefore it's relevant to **all companies dealing with the EU** (directly or via partners) and **all employees** - this includes **data controllers (gather data), processors (use data) and Data Protection Officers**. **Even post Brexit** the UK government plans alignment with GDPR.

Expert Recommendations:

In general and across all industries, GDPR experts are recommending **intensive training events for DPO's** and their companies, **tailored training events** for personal data handlers and general staff plus **online refreshers** for ongoing training and compliance documentation. **Independent auditing of compliance and internal tracking** of key compliance performance metrics is also recommended. **Documentation and prioritisation of risks are the key elements!**

Copyright © Maurice 'Big Mo' Flynn 2017-18 (Open Doors Ltd.)
GDPR Training Events - Reviews - Feedback

GDPR TRAINING AND AUDIT CHECKLIST

Subject	Last Completed	Next Date Planned (Qtrly/Annual)
DPO Training	Y/N Date:	Y/N Date:
Senior Management	Y/N Date:	Y/N Date:
Personal Data Handlers	Y/N Date:	Y/N Date:
All Staff and Partners	Y/N Date:	Y/N Date:
Board GDPR Performance Review	Y/N Date:	Y/N Date:
GDPR Compliance Audit	Y/N Date:	Y/N Date:

Document Control Reference: GDPR - Issue No:............... Issue Date:.............

Signature 1: Name:............Title:....Date:.....

Signature 2: Name:............Title:....Date:......

Copyright © Maurice 'Big Mo' Flynn 2017-18 (Open Doors Ltd.)
GDPR Training Events - Reviews - Feedback

Step 2: Complete data and risk audit

How?

Simply put, this means we need to **document all the personal data** we have and use, anywhere in our business or partner businesses. This personal data will be stored in a variety of places, including **official data storage facilities and informal places** e.g. on personal computers and mobile devices. It also means **non digital data** e.g. old reports and other documents. Just to reiterate we also need to include personal data that comes from or is shared **with business partners**. We need to **assess the GDPR compliance risks involved and plan to minimise.**

What's personal? [Video Link (00:53)]

Personal data is any data that can be used to **identify an individual person**. However it **doesn't just mean obvious stuff** like email addresses and mobile phone numbers. It includes **any** data that could be used to identify

Copyright © Maurice 'Big Mo' Flynn 2017-18 (Open Doors Ltd.)

someone <u>eg IP address and even pseudonyms.</u> For all personal data we need to record <u>what permission was given</u> for that data and <u>when it expires.</u> We also need to know <u>how the data can be found, shared, amended and deleted</u>.

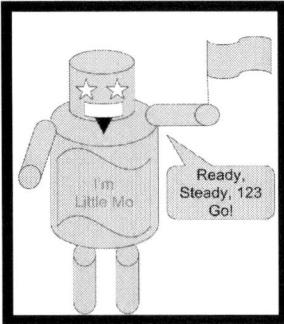

Expert Recommendations:

There is an <u>ongoing debate amongst experts</u> as to what extent <u>business contact information (B2B)</u> will be covered by GDPR. For now it's <u>safest to assume the worst</u> and plan for that, so that any "lightening" of the restrictions will be <u>a business upside!</u> (This is addressed in Art. 5,6,30 and 39).

Copyright © Maurice 'Big Mo' Flynn 2017-18 (Open Doors Ltd.)
GDPR Training Events - Reviews - Feedback

DATA AUDIT, FLOWS, RISK ASSESSMENT & GAP ANALYSIS

		Customers (Circle)	Prospects (Circle)	Employee (Circle)
Personal Data	1.Email 2.name 3.address 4.mobile phone 5.landline 6.IP address 7. other	1 2 3 4 5 6 7 =	1 2 3 4 5 6 7 =	1 2 3 4 5 6 7 =
Where From	1.Data subject 2.partner 3.other 3rd party 4.government 5.other	1 2 3 4 5 =	1 2 3 4 5=	1 2 3 4 5=
Legal Basis	1.Consent 2.contract 3.legal 4.legitimate 5.other	1 2 3 4 =	1 2 3 4 =	1 2 3 4 =
How Used	1.Communication 2.credit scoring 3.other profiling 4.payment 5.other.	1 2 3 4 5=	1 2 3 4 5=	1 2 3 4 5=
Who Uses	1.Marketing 2.sales 3.finance 4.IT 5.other	1 2 3 4 5=	1 2 3 4 5=	1 2 3 4 5=
Where Stored	1.Local server 2.cloud server 3.desktop/laptop 4.hardcopy 5.other	1 2 3 4 5=	1 2 3 4 5=	1 2 3 4 5=

Copyright © Maurice 'Big Mo' Flynn 2017-18 (Open Doors Ltd.)
GDPR Training Events - Reviews - Feedback

Who Shares?	1.Commercial partner 2.local government 3.national government 4.other	1 2 3 4 =	1 2 3 4 =	1 2 3 4 =
Risks	1.Firewall hack 2.email hack 3.lost device 4.internal hack 5.robbery 6.other	1 2 3 4 5 6=	1 2 3 4 5 6=	1 2 3 4 5 6=
Likelihood:	1.High 2.Medium 3.Low	1 2 3	1 2 3	1 2 3
Impact:	1.High 2.Medium 3.Low	1 2 3	1 2 3	1 2 3
Solution & Delivery Deadline	1.New firewall Q2 2.update patches Q1 3.email security training Q1 4.personal data training Q1	5.device data policy Q2 6.data access management Q2	7.general security and training Q2 9.GDPR risk dashboard	Q1 10.Key correspondence records Q2 11.New policy

Document Control Reference: GDPR - Issue No:................ Issue Date:.............

Signature 1: Name:............Title:....Date:.....

Signature 2: Name:............Title:....Date:......

Copyright © Maurice 'Big Mo' Flynn 2017-18 (Open Doors Ltd.)
GDPR Training Events - Reviews - Feedback

Step 3: Privacy policies

How?

There are new rules regarding **privacy notices, policies, rights and processes** that we all need to take into account. Businesses **need to first understand** these new requirements. Existing privacy notices need to be **amended (e.g. on your website) or new ones written in their absence**. All **employees and data sharing partners will need training** about the new rights and processes, to avoid risk of human error.

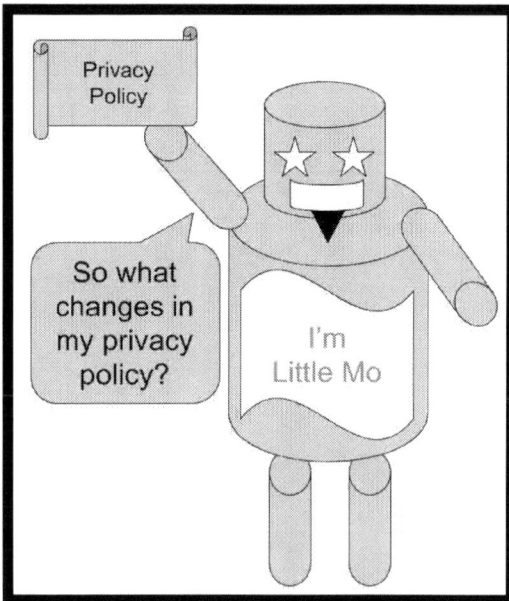

Privacy Policy

So what changes in my privacy policy?

I'm Little Mo

Copyright © Maurice 'Big Mo' Flynn 2017-18 (Open Doors Ltd.)
GDPR Training Events - Reviews - Feedback

The changes ... [Video Links 1 2]

Privacy policies and notices need to cover the **lawful basis** for collecting and processing personal data, plus **retention periods.** We also need to include the rights of the individual to **complain to the ICO, the right to be informed, to object, to access and rectify or erase, to restrict processing and automated decision-making** (eg profiling) plus **data portability** must all be simply explained.

Experts Recommendations:

Some of the **largest companies have been preparing for GDPR** for years so keep an eye out for how your favourite big brands (eg Google, Microsoft, supermarkets et al) are adjusting their policies as this way **you can get free learning, courtesy of their 'reams' of legal resource!**

(This is addressed in Art. 5,6,12-21,26,28 and 29).

Copyright © Maurice 'Big Mo' Flynn 2017-18 (Open Doors Ltd.)
GDPR Training Events - Reviews - Feedback

DATA PRIVACY NOTICE CHECKLIST

	Privacy Policy Translate Website	Mobile Friendly & Timely *100 words*	Phone & Verbal	Social Media Guide lines
Explains What Personal Data Is Used & How & Why It's Used	Y/N	Y/N	Y/N	Y/N
Explains How Long It's Used For & How It's Kept Secure	Y/N	Y/N	Y/N	Y/N
Explains Who Uses the Data ie Internal & External	Y/N	Y/N	Y/N	Y/N

Copyright © Maurice 'Big Mo' Flynn 2017-18 (Open Doors Ltd.)
GDPR Training Events - Reviews - Feedback

Explains the Legal Basis for Data Usage	Y/N	Y/N	Y/N	Y/N
Explains Your Rights eg Portability, Erase, Amend and Restrict Plus Contact Info	Y/N	Y/N	Y/N	Y/N
Easy To Find, Understand & Accessible	Y/N	Y/N	Y/N	Y/N

Document Control Reference: GDPR - Issue No:................ Issue Date:.............

Signature 1: Name:............Title:....Date:.....

Signature 2: Name:............Title:....Date:......

Copyright © Maurice 'Big Mo' Flynn 2017-18 (Open Doors Ltd.)
GDPR Training Events - Reviews - Feedback

Step 4: Prepare data requests

How?

Companies using personal data need to be ready to **respond at short notice** to data requests from the individual. Most companies **do not have the resources** or tools to do this reliably and **failure penalties are potentially high**. We need to first understand these new requirements and put in place the **people, processes and tools** to ensure compliance. All **employees and data sharing partners will need training** about the new processes to avoid risk of human error.

The requests ...
[Video Link]

Data requests from individuals can relate to any of the **rights mentioned in step 3 i.e. rights to object, be informed, access, rectify, erase, restrict processing and automated decision-**

Copyright © Maurice 'Big Mo' Flynn 2017-18 (Open Doors Ltd.)
GDPR Training Events - Reviews - Feedback

making plus portability. Companies have **one month (30 days) to respond** and **cannot charge** for these data requests, unless excessive. **If a company refuses**, it must **communicate why as well as the right to complain** for independent judgement eg via the ICO.

Expert Recommendations:

Responding to data requests is essential but few companies have the processes in place to comply reliably. **It's also hard to anticipate how many we might receive.** Smaller companies are tending to **set up manual processes** until the size of demand is clearer. Larger companies look to use **semi automated software tools** as probably the best scalable solution to use, especially when we're trying to **find all the data in multiple places**.

(This is addressed in Art. 6,12,15-22).

Copyright © Maurice 'Big Mo' Flynn 2017-18 (Open Doors Ltd.)
GDPR Training Events - Reviews - Feedback

SUBJECT ACCESS RECORD (SAR) REQUEST PROCESS

	Data Subject (Circle)	Legal Request (Circle)
Policy	Y/N	Y/N
30 Day Processes (Authenticate then 1.Inform 2.Access 3.Rectify 4.Erase 5.Restrict Process/Profiling 6.Portability 7.Objection)	1 2 3 4 5 6 7	Y/N
Documentation e.g.1.Form, 2.Letter Templates (Receipt, Clarification, Final Response - On/Offline)	1 2	Y/N

Copyright © Maurice 'Big Mo' Flynn 2017-18 (Open Doors Ltd.)
GDPR Training Events - Reviews - Feedback

Accessible	Y/N	Y/N
Tracking/Reporting	Y/N	Y/N
Multichannel	Y/N	Y/N
Automated? **Eg 1.Preference Centre 2.Customer Login 3. Customer Service Mailbox 4.Other**	Y/N 1 2 3 4 =	Y/N

Document Control Reference: GDPR - Issue No:............... Issue Date:............

Signature 1: Name:............Title:....Date:.....

Signature 2: Name:............Title:....Date:......

Copyright © Maurice 'Big Mo' Flynn 2017-18 (Open Doors Ltd.)
GDPR Training Events - Reviews - Feedback

Step 5: Lawful basis for data

How?

Companies holding and using personal data need to be be **clear on the lawful basis** for doing so and **document** that for evidencing on request. Companies can **no longer keep records of personal data indefinitely** or without detailed documentation as to why. **Individuals, supervisory bodies (the ICO) and courts** all can request access to that information at short notice. We need to first understand **what is permitted** under GDPR and put in place the **people, processes and tools** to ensure compliance. All **employees and data sharing partners will need training** about the new processes to avoid risk of human error.

Copyright © Maurice 'Big Mo' Flynn 2017-18 (Open Doors Ltd.)

It's the law dude ...
[Video Links 1 2 9:00]

Companies are permitted to hold and use personal data under any one of the following provisos. If **Consent** is given from the individual concerned; by **Contract** ie legal agreement; by **Law** if required eg employment law; if **Vital** eg for life-or-death scenarios; if for **Public** task eg courts; if **Legitimate Interests**, where we must **balance the legitimate interests and rights of all parties** e.g. the individual's **right to privacy** and businesses' **commercial need to communicate and find new solutions** to business challenges.

Copyright © Maurice 'Big Mo' Flynn 2017-18 (Open Doors Ltd.)
GDPR Training Events - Reviews - Feedback

Expert Recommendations:

Many companies have personal data captured over the years but with little or poor quality **documented consent.** Many companies have generalised databases where lot's of different **sources of data intermingle**. This all need to be untangled and **cleaned up fast**!

(This is addressed in Art. 5,6).

Copyright © Maurice 'Big Mo' Flynn 2017-18 (Open Doors Ltd.)
GDPR Training Events - Reviews - Feedback

LAWFUL BASIS RECORD

	Consent 1.Evidence 2.Timed (Circle)	Contract 1.Evidence 2.Timed (Circle)	Legitimate Interest 1.Evidence 2.Timed (Circle)
Customer Data	Y / N 1 2	Y / N 1 2	Y / N 1 2
Prospect Data	Y / N 1 2	Y / N 1 2	Y / N 1 2
Employee Data	Y / N 1 2	Y / N 1 2	Y / N 1 2
Partner Data	Y / N 1 2	Y / N 1 2	Y / N 1 2
Other Data	Y / N 1 2	Y / N 1 2	Y / N 1 2

Document Control Reference: GDPR - Issue No:............... Issue Date:.............

Signature 1: Name:............Title:....Date:.....

Signature 2: Name:............Title:....Date:......

Copyright © Maurice 'Big Mo' Flynn 2017-18 (Open Doors Ltd.)
GDPR Training Events - Reviews - Feedback

Step 6: Correct consent & legitimate use

How?

Many businesses use personal data which has been captured over months or years but with **poor quality consent documentation or legitimate use justification.** Many businesses have centralised databases where lots of different **sources of data intermingle**. All personal data that has not been correctly consented to must be re-assessed. We need to understand **what consent and legitimate use means under GDPR and audit our data accordingly**. Compliant data can be used for the **permitted time period. Non compliant data must be deleted or re-permissioned.**

Copyright © Maurice 'Big Mo' Flynn 2017-18 (Open Doors Ltd.)
GDPR Training Events - Reviews - Feedback

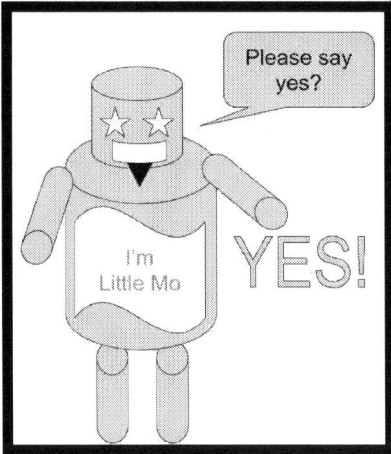

Was that a yes?
[Video Link 1]

Under GDPR consent must be **freely given, specific, informed and unambiguous.** It requires a positive opt-in i.e. it **cannot be inferred** via pre ticked boxes and must be definitive. Consent agreements must be **separate from other T&C's** i.e. not hidden. It also must be **simple to withdraw** consent at any time. Legitimate use means we must **balance the legitimate interests and rights of all parties** e.g. the individual's **right to privacy** and businesses' **commercial need to communicate and find new solutions** to business challenges.

Expert Recommendations:

Copyright © Maurice 'Big Mo' Flynn 2017-18 (Open Doors Ltd.)
GDPR Training Events - Reviews - Feedback

Many companies have personal data captured over the years with little or poor quality **documented consent and legitimate use justification.** Many companies have generalised databases where lots of different **sources of data intermingle**. This all need to be untangled and **cleaned up fast**!

(This is addressed in Art. 5,6 and 12).

Copyright © Maurice 'Big Mo' Flynn 2017-18 (Open Doors Ltd.)
GDPR Training Events - Reviews - Feedback

DOCUMENTING CONSENT & LEGITIMATE INTEREST

	Consent & Expiry	How Authenticate?	Legitimate Interest?
Prospect Data	x/x/20xx x/x/20xx	2 Factor eg Email, Web, Sms, Phone, Document? Y / N	1.Individual= xyz 2.Company= xyz
Partner Data	x/x/20xx x/x/20xx	2 Factor eg Email, Web, Sms, Phone, Document? Y / N	1.Individual= xyz 2.Company= xyz
Other Data	x/x/20xx x/x/20xx	2 Factor eg Email, Web, Sms, Phone, Document? Y / N	1.Individual= xyz 2.Company= xyz

Document Control Reference: GDPR - Issue No:............... Issue Date:.............

Signature 1: Name:............Title:....Date:.....

Signature 2: Name:............Title:....Date:......

Copyright © Maurice 'Big Mo' Flynn 2017-18 (Open Doors Ltd.)
GDPR Training Events - Reviews - Feedback

Step 7: Rules for children and other sensitive data

How?

As you might expect **childrens' and other sensitive data merits extra protection** although it **can vary by country**. The main issue for kids is **from whom the consent permission** came and **are they old enough** to be legally responsible? For sensitive data (e.g. race or ethnic origin, politics, religion, trade union status, health, sex preference, criminal record) we can **only use it in restricted ways**. Sensitive data has also been extended to include genetic data and biometric data. We need to understand **what consent for children means under GDPR and audit our data accordingly.** We also need to be clear on **how other sensitive data can be used**. Compliant data can be used for the **permitted time period. Non compliant data must be deleted or re-checked eg for permission or another lawful basis.**

Copyright © Maurice 'Big Mo' Flynn 2017-18 (Open Doors Ltd.)
GDPR Training Events - Reviews - Feedback

How old are you?

In the UK it is proposed that under GDPR children can give their own consent to personal data usage **at 13 years and above although this has still not completed Parliamentary approval**. Other countries will set the age limit **between 13-16 years** and are also finalising their plans. Under these age limits consent must be obtained from the **parent or legal guardian**. Sensitive data use (eg health, ethnicity, criminal records et al) **must comply with all existing restrictions (e.g. minimised use for lawful tasks) with added transparency under GDPR. Public bodies cannot rely on "legitimate interest." Criminal record data usage is further restricted.**

Expert Recommendations:

Copyright © Maurice 'Big Mo' Flynn 2017-18 (Open Doors Ltd.)
GDPR Training Events - Reviews - Feedback

One of the key challenges here is the **different treatment of children by age of consent across countries**. For sensitive data **specialist advice is recommended if this is a big part of the business model.** (This is addressed in Art. 8,9 and 10).

Copyright © Maurice 'Big Mo' Flynn 2017-18 (Open Doors Ltd.)
GDPR Training Events - Reviews - Feedback

Step 8: Data breach response

How?

Until now companies have often **kept quiet about data breaches, hacks and leaks** as there was little incentive to go public but that's all changing. We now need to **report personal data breaches very quickly or risk big fines**. Most companies recognise they don't currently have the people, processes or tools to do this scalably.

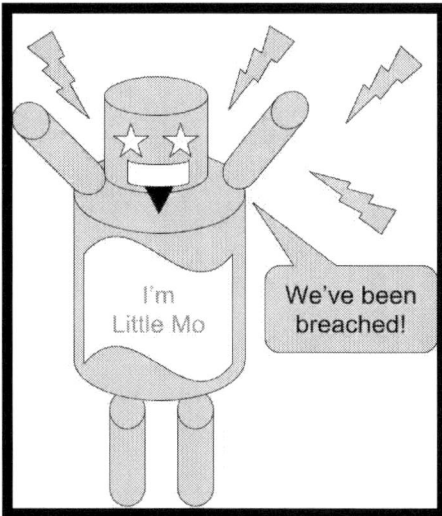

We need to first understand **what is required** under GDPR and put in place the **people, processes and tools** to ensure compliance. All **employees and data sharing partners will need training** about the new processes to avoid risk of human error.

Copyright © Maurice 'Big Mo' Flynn 2017-18 (Open Doors Ltd.)
GDPR Training Events - Reviews - Feedback

What to do? [Video Link]

Personal data breaches must be reported to the Information Commissioner's Office (ico.org.uk) **within 72 hours** or we risk fines of up to 20m Euro's or 4% global turnover, whichever is larger! Data breaches must also be reported to the individuals involved without delay if "high risk" ie **if likely to risk the rights of individuals eg via discrimination, reputation, financial loss, loss of confidentiality** **or any other significant economic or social disadvantage.**

Expert Recommendations:

Imagine trying to deal manually with a data breach at **midnight on 25th December** or other big national holidays! Smaller companies are tending to **set up manual processes** to prepare cost effectively. Larger companies are looking to use **semi automated software tools** as probably the best scalable solution.

(This is addressed in Art. 12 and 33).

Copyright © Maurice 'Big Mo' Flynn 2017-18 (Open Doors Ltd.)
GDPR Training Events - Reviews - Feedback

DATA BREACH RECORD CHECKLIST

Policy	Y / N
72 Hour Process: 1.Qualify and Quantify 2.Confirm 3. Inform Internal 4.Inform ICO 5.Assess Risk & Inform Subject 6.Rectify 7.Review & Future Proof	1 2 3 4 5 6 7
Documentation eg Forms, Letter Templates	Y / N
Accessibility & Multichannel - Tracking - Automated	Y / N Y / N - Y / N

Document Control Reference: GDPR - Issue No:................ Issue Date:.............

Signature 1: Name:............Title:....Date:.....

Signature 2: Name:............Title:....Date:......

Copyright © Maurice 'Big Mo' Flynn 2017-18 (Open Doors Ltd.)
GDPR Training Events - Reviews - Feedback

Step 9: Protection by design

How?

Many companies have as many data leakage risks as an old watering can has water leaks! **Employees roam the world accessing and sharing personal data on a variety of devices and systems** only some of which are secure. GDPR means this cannot continue. A better approach means **rethinking personal data usage** in your company and **ensuring it cannot leak by design** rather than by accident. Most companies recognise they don't currently have the people, processes or tools **to do this scalably**. We need to first understand **what is required** under GDPR and put in place the **people, processes and tools** to ensure compliance.

Copyright © Maurice 'Big Mo' Flynn 2017-18 (Open Doors Ltd.)
GDPR Training Events - Reviews - Feedback

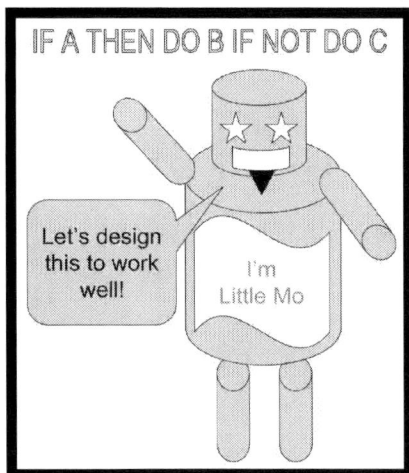

By design?
[Video Link]

Protection by design means building privacy into every process and system **from the ground up** and from scratch if needed. We can **map the flows of data** and **cut out areas of risk** eg human error. To get there we need to **minimise & delete, protect, anonymise, pseudonymise & encrypt, inform, give_access & automate**.

Data Protection Impact Assessments are for new, high risk areas e.g. new projects and data transfers. **Within 8 weeks of submitting a DPIA** (plus an additional 6 weeks may be required for complex cases), the supervisory authority (i.e. in the UK this is the ICO) **will give advice on whether the intended project has GDPR issues.**

Copyright © Maurice 'Big Mo' Flynn 2017-18 (Open Doors Ltd.)
GDPR Training Events - Reviews - Feedback

Expert Recommendations:

For big companies with large amounts of data **this is a big set of changes and requirements - see example checklist overleaf**. For smaller companies **this is less onerous - see underlined elements overleaf.**

(This is addressed in Art.5,24,25 and 32).

Copyright © Maurice 'Big Mo' Flynn 2017-18 (Open Doors Ltd.)
GDPR Training Events - Reviews - Feedback

PRIVACY BY DESIGN CHECKLIST

Integrated with InfoSec Policy eg ISO270001	Y / N
Data classification procedure	Y / N
Encryption technology and processes	Y / N
Identity Access Management (need to know basis)	Y / N
Software tools for aggregation, data masking, pseudonymisation, and anonymisation	Y / N
Policy and procedure on pseudonymisation or anonymization	Y / N
Enterprise privacy risk assessment and mitigation plan	Y / N
Audits of methodology	Y / N
Record retention policy	Y / N
Application development protocols	Y / N
Project security risk assessments	Y / N

Copyright © Maurice 'Big Mo' Flynn 2017-18 (Open Doors Ltd.)
GDPR Training Events - Reviews - Feedback

Security of processing	Y / N
Perimeter security measures	Y / N
System monitoring	Y / N
Acceptable use policy	Y / N
Information security audit of system access privileges	Y / N Y / N
Password parameters	
Data center security measures (e.g., biometrics, access restriction, monitoring)	Y / N
Electronic badge access system - Physical records room with locked doors	Y / N Y / N
Restricted access to backup tapes and media	Y / N
Clean desk policy	Y / N
Employee agreement outlines security	Y / N

Copyright © Maurice 'Big Mo' Flynn 2017-18 (Open Doors Ltd.)
GDPR Training Events - Reviews - Feedback

responsibilities	Y / N
Employee termination checklist	
Employee background checks	Y / N
Data loss prevention (DLP) software	Y / N
Data privacy and security requirements for third parties	Y / N
	Y / N
Contracts with third parties processing data	Y / N
Business continuity plan	Y / N
Job descriptions for data protection-related roles	Y / N
Contract templates for DPO functions (if outsourcing)	Y / N
	Y / N
Defined privacy roles and responsibilities	Y / N
Privacy steering committee	Y / N
Data protection training and awareness materials	Y / N

Copyright © Maurice 'Big Mo' Flynn 2017-18 (Open Doors Ltd.)
GDPR Training Events - Reviews - Feedback

Data protection as a regular agenda-item for the board	Y / N
Data protection impact assessment templates	Y / N
Data protection impact assessment guidelines	Y / N
Budget for the DPO function	Y / N
Policy on conflict of interests	Y / N
Formal reporting structures	Y / N
Procedures for handling inquiries and complaints	Y / N
Data privacy notice	Y / N
Procedures or guidance on when to seek DPO input	Y / N
Document Control Procedure GDPR	Y / N
Data Protection Policy Review Procedure GDPR	Y / N
Contact with Authorities Work Instruction	Y / N

Copyright © Maurice 'Big Mo' Flynn 2017-18 (Open Doors Ltd.)
GDPR Training Events - Reviews - Feedback

Storage Removal Procedure	Y / N
Third Party Contracts	Y / N
External Parties – Information Security Procedure	Y / N
<u>Reporting Information Security Weaknesses and Events Procedure</u>	Y / N
Responding to Information Security Reports	Y / N
Collection of Evidence Procedure	Y / N
Control of Records Procedure	Y / N
Monitor and Measurement Register	Y / N
Audit Schedule	Y / N
Audit Lead Report Sheet	Y / N
Management Review Record	
Schedule of Authorities and Key Suppliers	

Copyright © Maurice 'Big Mo' Flynn 2017-18 (Open Doors Ltd.)
GDPR Training Events - Reviews - Feedback

Removal of Information Assets Information Security Event Reports	

Document Control Reference: GDPR - Issue No:............... Issue Date:.............

Signature 1: Name:............Title:....Date:.....

Signature 2: Name:............Title:....Date:......

Copyright © Maurice 'Big Mo' Flynn 2017-18 (Open Doors Ltd.)
GDPR Training Events - Reviews - Feedback

DATA PROTECTION IMPACT ASSESSMENT

What is the aim and description of the project?	
What personal data will be collected?	
How will the personal data be collected?	
Where will the personal data be stored?	
Where will the personal data be shared?	
How will the personal data be amended or deleted?	
GDPR risks identified (individual, organisational, compliance)?	
Solutions identified (individual, organisational, compliance)?	
Other safeguards, security measures and mechanisms to ensure compliance?	

Document Control Reference: GDPR - Issue No:................ Issue Date:.............

Signature 1: Name:............Title:....Date:.....

Signature 2: Name:............Title:....Date:......

Copyright © Maurice 'Big Mo' Flynn 2017-18 (Open Doors Ltd.)
GDPR Training Events - Reviews - Feedback

Step 10: Data protection officer

Must We?

Bigger companies (250+ employees) using lots of personal data are **compelled to have a data protection officer**. Smaller companies are not be but the principles of the role help **avoid some of the risks** associated with GDPR compliance **eg ownership/ responsibility**. Companies need to assess the mandatories and risks and **look at in house vs outsourced requirements.**

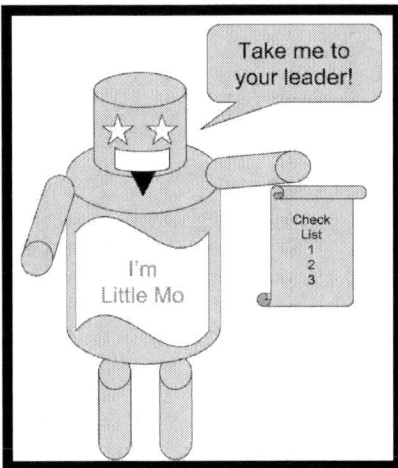

Copyright © Maurice 'Big Mo' Flynn 2017-18 (Open Doors Ltd.)
GDPR Training Events - Reviews - Feedback

Tell me officer?

[Video Links 1 0:07 2 0:14]

A DPO is mandatory for **public bodies, large users of sensitive data or if you undertake large scale, regular and systematic monitoring of data subjects.** Many larger companies also find it the best way to manage the GDPR risks and processes and **ensure ownership**. The DPO should be a data privacy law **expert;** advise the Controller or Processor and its employees of **data protection obligations**; monitor **compliance, including assigning responsibilities**, training and audits; advise on and monitor **DPIA impact assessments**, cooperate with and contact the **supervisory authority and data subjects** as required; be involved in **all issues** relating to processing personal data; ensure **sufficient resources**, act in an **independent** manner, with direct reporting to the **highest management level.** It is not a role to be allocated lightly.

Copyright © Maurice 'Big Mo' Flynn 2017-18 (Open Doors Ltd.)
GDPR Training Events - Reviews - Feedback

Expert Recommendations:

For larger companies having a DPO **ensures ownership** of the responsibilities of GDPR compliance. **In house if resources allow but can be contracted if resources/expertise lacking.**

For smaller companies there may not be enough work for a full time DPO. **In this case a well resourced cross functional team, with a clearly identified team leader plus senior management sponsorship, should suffice.**

(This is addressed in Art.38 and 39).

Copyright © Maurice 'Big Mo' Flynn 2017-18 (Open Doors Ltd.)
GDPR Training Events - Reviews - Feedback

Step 11: International preparation

Where?

The EU's governing bodies **want to deal with local contacts** when it comes to issues of GDPR compliance so companies will have to select and document who and where that is (called your **"lead data protection supervisory authority"**). Employees and partners should **also be made aware. Personal data transfers to countries outside the EU and a short list of approved countries** are also restricted.

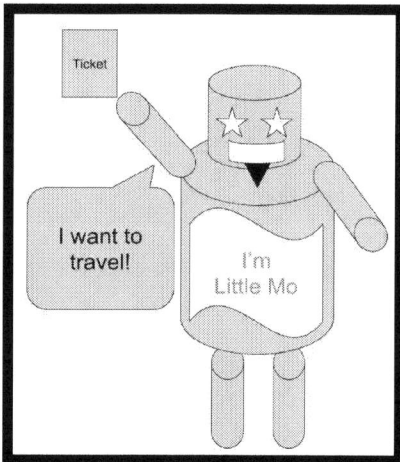

Around the world?
[Video Links 1 9:19 2]

Your lead data protection supervisory authority is your supervisory authority

Copyright © Maurice 'Big Mo' Flynn 2017-18 (Open Doors Ltd.)
GDPR Training Events - Reviews - Feedback

in the state where your main establishment is. Your main establishment is your **EU central administration or the location where data decisions are made.** Personal data transfers between countries and outside the EU **must be made under certain secure, approved processes only - see overleaf.**

Expert Recommendation:

For UK companies your lead office will be **UK HQ until after Brexit.** For European companies this will be **European HQ** most of the time, unless local factors intervene. **Data transfer rules** are still under debate in some areas - see overleaf.

(This is addressed in Art.27 and 45-49).

Copyright © Maurice 'Big Mo' Flynn 2017-18 (Open Doors Ltd.)
GDPR Training Events - Reviews - Feedback

INTERNATIONAL DATA TRANSFER PROCESS

	Y/N
1. Is the personal data transfer within EU?	Y/N
2. Is personal data transfer to country with "adequate data protection laws"? e.g. Canada, Switzerland (http://ec.europa.eu/justice/data-protection/international-transfers/adequacy/index_en.htm)	Y/N
3. Is personal data transfer with USA under EU-US Privacy Shield? (NB Ongoing issues.)	Y/N
4. Is personal data transfer using Binding corporate rules BCR's and/or legal contracts?	Y/N

Document Control Reference: GDPR - Issue No:............... Issue Date:.............

Signature 1: Name:............Title:....Date:.....

Signature 2: Name:............Title:....Date:......

Copyright © Maurice 'Big Mo' Flynn 2017-18 (Open Doors Ltd.)
GDPR Training Events - Reviews - Feedback

Step 12: Plan of attack

How?

Big companies have been preparing for GDPR for years. Some **smaller companies** haven't started. It's not too late of course but we all need to **start now and focus on the priorities.**

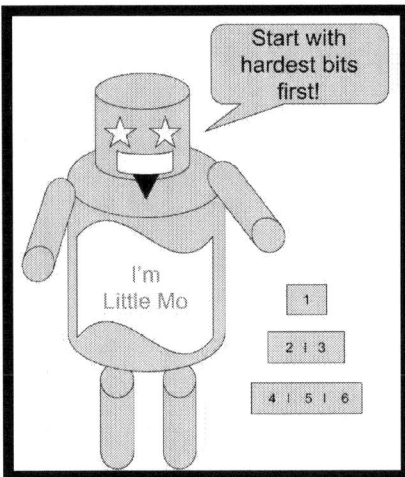

Let's Prioritise!

The key elements for attacking GDPR prep with speed and accuracy are generally agreed to be the following:

1. A cross functional Data Privacy Steering Committee with a board level sponsor and expert external partners if needed;

Copyright © Maurice 'Big Mo' Flynn 2017-18 (Open Doors Ltd.)
GDPR Training Events - Reviews - Feedback

2. Data audit, risks, gaps and data flow analysis;

3. Project timeline, resources and tools;

4. Data protection and privacy policy i.e. summary of all the previous sections, tailored for your business.

Expert Recommendations:

This does not have to be too difficult if you **start today & prioritise!**

Copyright © Maurice 'Big Mo' Flynn 2017-18 (Open Doors Ltd.)
GDPR Training Events - Reviews - Feedback

PROJECT PLANNING

Prep Steps	Risk Level (Circle)	Resource Level (Circle)	Leadtimes Estimate (Mths) (Circle)
1 Awareness	**High** / Medium / Low	High / Medium / **Low**	**1-2** / 3-4 / 5+
2 Audit	**High** / Medium / Low	**High** / Medium / Low	1-2 / **3-4** / 5+
3 Privacy Policy	**High** / Medium / Low	High / **Medium** / Low	1-2 / **3-4** / 5+
4 Requests	**High** / Medium / Low	High / **Medium** / Low	1-2 / **3-4** / 5+
5 Lawful Basis	**High** / Medium / Low	High / **Medium** / Low	1-2 / 3-4 / **5+**
6 Consent/Legit	**High** / Medium / Low	**High** / Medium / Low	1-2 / 3-4 / **5+**
7 Kids & Sensitive Data	High / **Medium** / Low	High / **Medium** / Low	1-2 / 3-4 / **5+**
8 Data Breach	**High** / Medium / Low	High / **Medium** / Low	1-2 / **3-4** / 5+
9 Privacy By Design / DPIA	High / **Medium** / Low	**High** / Medium / Low	1-2 / 3-4 / **5+**
10 DPO	High / **Medium** / Low	**High** / Medium / Low	1-2 / 3-4 / **5+**
11 International	High / **Medium** / Low	**High** / Medium / Low	1-2 / 3-4 / **5+**
12 Plan	**High** / Medium / Low	**High** / Medium / Low	1-2 / **3-4** / 5+

Document Control Reference: GDPR - Issue No:................ Issue Date:.............

Signature 1: Name:............Title:....Date:.....

Signature 2: Name:............Title:....Date:......

Copyright © Maurice 'Big Mo' Flynn 2017-18 (Open Doors Ltd.)
GDPR Training Events - Reviews - Feedback

Content

Copyright © Maurice 'Big Mo' Flynn 2017-18 (Open Doors Ltd.)
GDPR Training Events - Reviews - Feedback

Copyright © Maurice 'Big Mo' Flynn 2017-18 (Open Doors Ltd.)
GDPR Training Events - Reviews - Feedback

Part 2 - Optimise Digital Channels in a Post GDPR World

Whazzup?

Now that we're **up to speed with GDPR compliance**, let's take a look at our **digital channels and how we can optimise** those further. **Some of this is quite advanced** on the assumption most companies have been using these channels for years but in all cases there are **simple improvements outlined that we can all benefit from as well as intermediate and advanced steps**. We will **focus on areas of most relevance to all.**

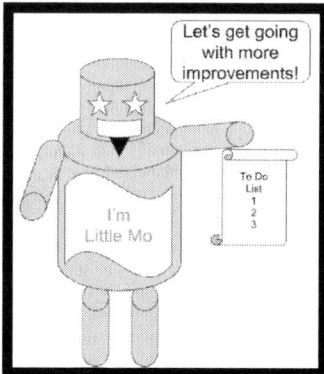

How can we all improve?

[Video Link 1]

My key digital channels are ... ?:

Copyright © Maurice 'Big Mo' Flynn 2017-18 (Open Doors Ltd.)
GDPR Training Events - Reviews - Feedback

Expert Recommendations:

Based on my work with 100's of companies, **most companies digital channels can be significantly improved in 4 areas which are: Reach, Cadence, Personalisation and Social Shares.** I'll explain these areas in the context of the different digital channels and the content we should use there.

Copyright © Maurice 'Big Mo' Flynn 2017-18 (Open Doors Ltd.)
GDPR Training Events - Reviews - Feedback

2.1 Email CRM automation and databases

How?

There are several key ways to better engage customers and stakeholders: **Reach i.e % of target audience, Cadence i.e. timing, Personalisation and activating Social Sharing**. Most marketers **don't pull all these levers** to the max and don't automate enough for **scalability**. Over the years email has been seen as a **niche tool** and it's also been **too profitable** for its own good. **Confusion over permission** hasn't helped. As a marketing practice it needs to **grow up and take its rightful leading place** at the business table. Email is a **key identifier** for the digital age - this has pro's and con's of course. Companies need to ensure their strategy is mature and **integrated.**

So where do we start?

I'm Little Mo

Four areas of improvement:

'Big Mo' Flynn 2017-18 (Open Doors Ltd.)
Training Events - Reviews - Feedback

<u>Reach</u> - How can I find more of my targets eg via email?

<u>Cadence</u> - How do I decide the optimum send frequency and time?

<u>Personalisation</u> - What's the right content and why?

<u>Social</u> - How can I motivate sharing?

Expert Recommendations:

- ☒ Big Mo's **<u>eCRM Improvement Grid</u>**: See below.

- ☒ **Example Video Links:** <u>Apparel</u> - <u>Charity</u> - <u>Engineering</u> - <u>Media/Events</u> - <u>MicroSME</u> - <u>Retail/Ecommerce</u> - <u>Pharma/Healthcare</u> - <u>Telco</u> - <u>Legal</u> - <u>Travel</u> - <u>Property</u> - <u>ITC</u>

Copyright © Maurice 'Big Mo' Flynn 2017-18 (Open Doors Ltd.)
<u>GDPR Training Events</u> - <u>Reviews</u> - <u>Feedback</u>

Big Mo's eCRM Improvement Grid:

TARGET	1.Reach	2. Cadence	3.Personalise
NEED	Data Partners	Time of send analysis + control tools.	Personalisation analysis + control tools.
TOOLS	Data Partners: Experian / Creditsafe / Acxiom (use Test Samples)	Via Email Service Provider or use Excel + Extension Library (Predictive Analytics)	ESP Via Partner (App) Library (eg Altaire.com)
FINANCE ANALYSIS	Excel + Predictive Analytics Extension	Excel + Predictive Analytics Extension	Excel + Predictive Analytics Extension
EXAMPLE	Sport/Bet, All Retail, Travel, Finance, B2B, SME, Other	Sport/Bet, All Retail, Travel, Finance, B2B, SME, Other	Sport/Bet, All Retail, Travel, Finance, B2B, SME, Other

Copyright © Maurice 'Big Mo' Flynn 2017-18 (Open Doors Ltd.)
GDPR Training Events - Reviews - Feedback

2.2 Content creation inc PR crisis comms

Latest Insights

We never have enough content right? **Yet we all create content all day long** when we speak to people, share opinions, write emails, post on Facebook and even show stuff with our hands and facial gestures. However when it comes to content creation for digital channels **all too often we panic** and think it's too hard, time consuming or risky.

So What To Do?

My approach is to capture more of the day to day content that is created in every business and **use simple tools to spin that rough stuff into content gold**!

Expert Recommendations:

Copyright © Maurice 'Big Mo' Flynn 2017-18 (Open Doors Ltd.)
GDPR Training Events - Reviews - Feedback

- Big Mo's **Content Improvement Grid**: See Below.

- **Example Video Links: Charity**

Copyright © Maurice 'Big Mo' Flynn 2017-18 (Open Doors Ltd.)
GDPR Training Events - Reviews - Feedback

Big Mo's Content Improvement Grid:

CONTENT	1. Text / Images	2.Audio/Video /Animation	3.Crisis
NEED	Audio tran scription & auto generation - screen capture	Easy to use video/audio /animation tools	Replace ment content on dark sites
FREEMIUM TOOLS	Youtube MTurk Wordsmith Jing Giphy EnhanceNet	Animoto GHangout Youtube Enhance	Wordpress 1Wordpres s2 Pre crisis rehearse - Post crisis - see SEO
FINANCIAL ANALYSIS	Excel + Predictive Analytics Extension	Excel + Predictive Analytics Extension	Excel + Predictive Analytics Extension
EXAMPLES	Marketing agencies	Marketing agencies	British Council

Copyright © Maurice 'Big Mo' Flynn 2017-18 (Open Doors Ltd.)
GDPR Training Events - Reviews - Feedback

2.3 Twitter, Facebook, LinkedIn, other social & ads

Latest Insights

Social media seems to have **taken over the world** at times - from elections to legal debates to celebrity culture and everything in between. The dominant platforms have **become mainstream** - the newer platforms will **often be bought up** before they can compete or alternatively drowned out. Of course the younger generation will always seek the **new, lower cost channels**.

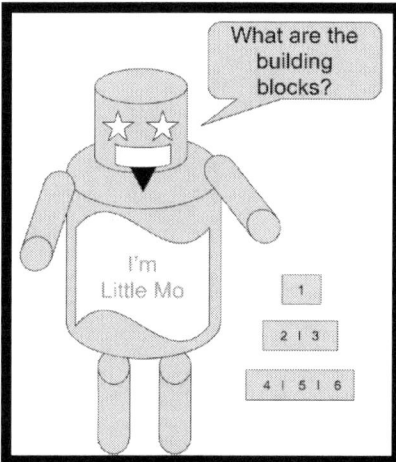

Copyright © Maurice 'Big Mo' Flynn 2017-18 (Open Doors Ltd.)
GDPR Training Events - Reviews - Feedback

OK What Now?

Nowadays I look at social media as **simply more channels** for dialogue and engagement so the **questions to consider** become: are **your customers and stakeholders** there and if so what, if anything, **might they want from you there?** We need to download our data from social media platforms so we can **analyse it better and understand which content really works well i.e.drives commercial value and ROI**. Ads online allow you to boost your reach **once you know what the commercial value is.**

Expert Recommendation:

- ☐ Big Mo's **Social Improvement Grid**: See below.
- ☐ Example Video Links: Property1 2 3 4 5 6

Copyright © Maurice 'Big Mo' Flynn 2017-18 (Open Doors Ltd.)

Big Mo's Social Improvement Grid:

PLATFORM	Facebook Twitter	LinkedIn	Other	Ads
NEED	Analyse better what drives more positive engagement	Analyse better what drives more positive engagement	Analyse better what drives more positive engageme nt	Amplify success
TOOLS	Extract data via FacebookApps or SimplyMeasure d & Trackur	Extract data via Hootsuite	Test and learn via Pinterest Snapchat Whatsapp	FacebookA ds GAdwords AmazonAd s
FINANCIAL ANALYSIS	Excel + Predictive Analytics Extension	Excel + Predictive Analytics Extension	Excel + Predictive Analytics Extension	Excel + Predictive Analytics Extension
EXAMPLE	Sport/Bet, All Retail, Travel, Finance, B2B, SME, Other	Marketing Agencies	Marketing Agencies	Sport/Bet, All Retail, Travel, Finance, B2B, SME, Other

Copyright © Maurice 'Big Mo' Flynn 2017-18 (Open Doors Ltd.)
GDPR Training Events - Reviews - Feedback

2.4 Websites, blogs, apps and search engine optimisation

Latest Insights

We'll focus again here on key drivers of customer and

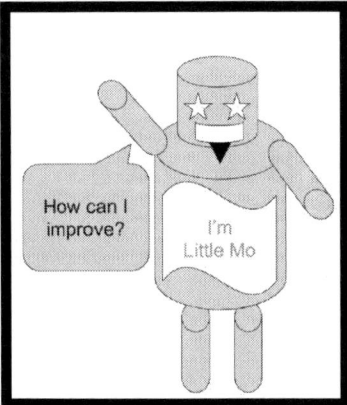

stakeholder growth and satisfaction: **reach, cadence, personalisation and social shares**. To do this best we need to **solve people's problems and answer their questions**, in a quick and engaging style. **Websites** need to personalise more, **blogs** need to share more and **apps** are for loyalty if needed. SEO will change a lot with **audio, visual and even AI search** so let's get the **basics right first**.

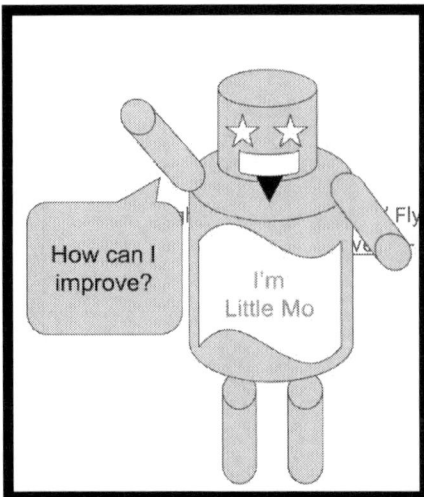

Flynn 2017-18 (Open Doors Ltd.)

Areas of improvement:

- ☒ **Reach** - How can I find more of my targets eg via SEO?
- ☒ **Cadence & Personalisation** - What's the right content & when? How do I personalise? What are apps best for?

Expert Recommendation:

- ☒ Big Mo's **Web Improvement Grid**: See below.

- ☒ **Video Link Examples:** SME Property 1 2 3 4 5 6 7 8 9 10

Copyright © Maurice 'Big Mo' Flynn 2017-18 (Open Doors Ltd.)

Big Mo's Web Improvement Grid:

TARGET	Reach	Cadence	Personalise
NEED	SEO improvement based on data analytics	Web/blog improvement via personalisation analysis	App based on personalisation
TOOLS & PARTNERS	Keyword lists & rankings via GTrends Adwords Moz	Web CMS with login or content personalisation tools eg DECCO	App with login eg via Codeless and/or use notifications gateway
FINANCE ANALYSIS	Excel + Predictive Analytics Extension	Excel + Predictive Analytics Extension	Excel + Predictive Analytics Extension
EXAMPLES	Marketing Agencies	Sport/Bet, All Retail, Travel, Finance, B2B, SME, Other	Sport/Bet, All Retail, Travel, Finance, B2B, SME, Other

Copyright © Maurice 'Big Mo' Flynn 2017-18 (Open Doors Ltd.)
GDPR Training Events - Reviews - Feedback

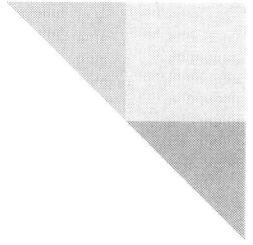

Copyright © Maurice 'Big Mo' Flynn 2017-18 (Open Doors Ltd.)
GDPR Training Events - Reviews - Feedback

2.5 The future and future proofing

Trends "as big as the web"...

1. Machine learning.

2. Machine vision and audio eg Alexa, Tesla et al.

3. Blockchain for contracts and cryptocurrency.

Only one certainty ... continuous, ever faster change!

So be adaptable to survive and hopefully thrive!

Who proved that first? Darwin wasn't it ... ?

Plus ca change .. plus c'est le meme chose!

A bientot! :)

Copyright © Maurice 'Big Mo' Flynn 2017-18 (Open Doors Ltd.)
GDPR Training Events - Reviews - Feedback

2.6 Appendix A

Useful Links:

https://gdpr-info.eu

https://www.youtube.com/watch?v=KzM-XLwgfAc

https://www.alienvault.com/blogs/security-essentials/are-businesses-prepared-for-gdpr

https://vimeo.com/230965114

https://www.youtube.com/watch?v=xIW5RI8K3Yg

https://www.youtube.com/watch?v=Ezdxg4vgAio

https://www.oracle.com/uk/corporate/features/gdpr.html?bcid=5584974298001&playerType=single-social&size=w01&shareUrl=http://www.oracle.com#close

https://vimeo.com/196298299

https://www.youtube.com/watch?v=PToCYQ-cxwk

https://www.youtube.com/watch?v=Vxsu2NMF3vM

Copyright © Maurice 'Big Mo' Flynn 2017-18 (Open Doors Ltd.)
GDPR Training Events - Reviews - Feedback

https://www.youtube.com/watch?v=PzHZVcWsKvU

https://www.youtube.com/watch?v=1J2rX2Km6Nc

https://www.youtube.com/watch?v=PWa8-43kE-Q&t=16s

https://trends.google.co.uk/trends/

https://adwords.google.com/home/

https://moz.com/tools/rank-tracker

http://www.decco-engine.com

https://www.codelessplatforms.com

https://support.google.com/youtube/answer/6373554?hl=en

https://www.mturk.com

http://wordsmith.readme.io/v1.5/docs

https://www.techsmith.com/jing-tool.html

https://giphy.com

http://webdav.tuebingen.mpg.de/pixel/enhancenet/

Copyright © Maurice 'Big Mo' Flynn 2017-18 (Open Doors Ltd.)
GDPR Training Events - Reviews - Feedback

https://animoto.com

https://hangouts.google.com

https://support.google.com/youtube/answer/1388383

https://wordpress.org

https://wordpress.com

https://www.youtube.com/watch?v=c1l86Gw8dGo

http://www.trackur.com/quick-start

https://developers.facebook.com/apps

https://www.youtube.com/watch?v=Xwx_Lc_pRsl

https://www.facebook.com/business/products/ads

https://advertising.amazon.co.uk

Copyright © Maurice 'Big Mo' Flynn 2017-18 (Open Doors Ltd.)
GDPR Training Events - Reviews - Feedback

Index

Copyright © Maurice 'Big Mo' Flynn 2017-18 (Open Doors Ltd.)
GDPR Training Events - Reviews - Feedback

Copyright © Maurice 'Big Mo' Flynn 2017-18 (Open Doors Ltd.)
GDPR Training Events - Reviews - Feedback

How to Prepare for GDPR and Improve Digital Channels in a Post GDPR World

An introductory summary by:

Maurice 'Big Mo' Flynn FCIM CMPRCA MEng Cantab

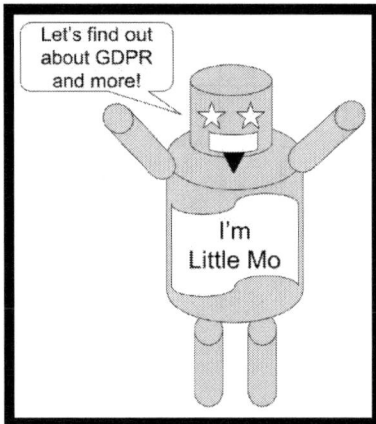

Copyright © Maurice 'Big Mo' Flynn 2017-18 (Open Doors Ltd.)
GDPR Training Events - Reviews - Feedback

27821215R00046

Printed in Great Britain
by Amazon